Reading/Writing Companion

McGraw Hill

mheducation.com/prek-12

Send all inquiries to:
McGraw Hill
1325 Avenue of the Americas
New York, NY 10019

ISBN: 978-1-26-573255-4
MHID: 1-26-573255-8

Printed in the United States of America.

3 4 5 6 7 8 9 LMN 26 25 24 23 22

A

Welcome to WONDERS!

We are so excited about how much you will learn and grow this year! We're here to help you set goals for your learning.

You will build on what you already know and learn new things every day.

You will read a lot of fun stories and interesting texts on different topics.

You will write about the texts you read. You will also write texts of your own. You will do research as well.

You will explore new ideas by reading different texts.

Each week, we will set goals on the My Goals page. Here is an example:

I can read and understand texts.

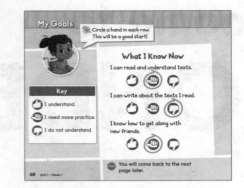

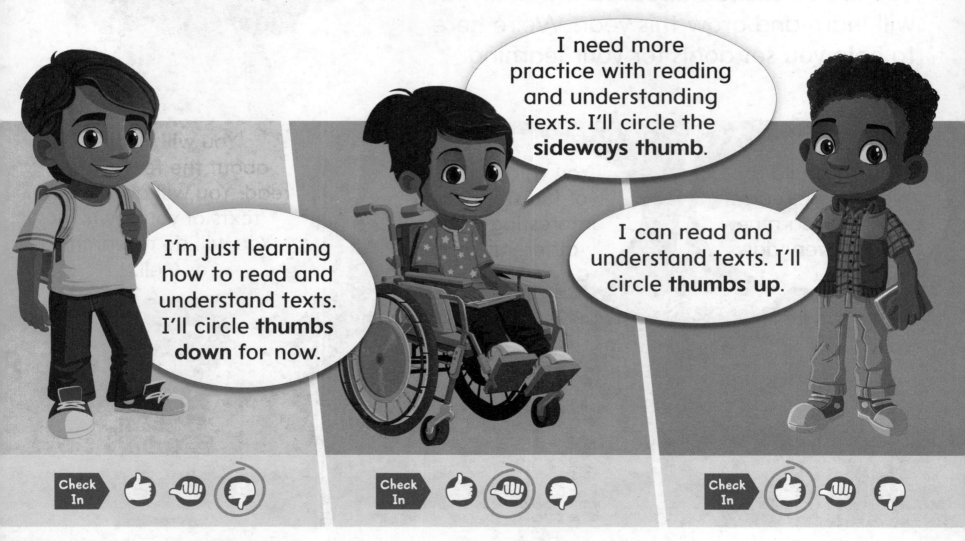

As you read and write, you will learn skills and strategies to help you reach your goals.

You will think about your learning and sometimes circle a hand to show your progress.

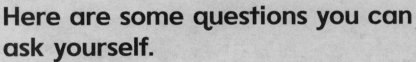

Here are some questions you can ask yourself.

- Did I understand the task?

- Was it easy?

- Was it hard?

- What made it hard?

It is okay if I need more practice. The most important thing is to do my best and keep learning!

If you need more help, you can choose what to do.

- Talk to a friend or teacher.
- Use an Anchor Chart.
- Choose a center activity.

At the end of each week, you will complete a fun task to show what you have learned.

Then you will return to your My Goals page and think about your learning.

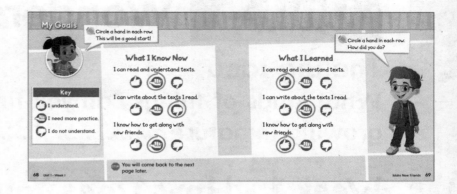

Unit 5 Wonders of Nature

The Big Idea
What kinds of things can you find
growing in nature?

Week 1 • How Does Your Garden Grow?

Literature Big Book *My Garden*

Shared Read "Hop Can Hop!"

Paired Selection Poetry About Plants

Digital Tools Find this eBook and other resources at: **my.mheducation.com**

Week 2 • Trees

SCIENCE

Janette Hill/Alamy

Week 3 • Fresh from the Farm

Unit 5

Wonders of Nature

The Big Idea What kinds of things can you find growing in nature?

....

 Talk about what you see in the picture. Speak in a loud, clear voice. Use correct grammar, too.

 Circle things that are growing.

Build Knowledge

Build Vocabulary

 Talk about what living things need to grow. What words tell about what living things need to grow?

 Draw a picture of one of the words.

 Write the word.

My Goals

 Circle a hand in each row.
It will be fun to learn more.

What I Know Now

I can read and understand texts.

I can write about the texts I read.

I know what living things need to grow.

Key

 I understand.

 I need more practice.

 I do not understand.

 You will come back to the next page later.

The setting is

_____

- -

_____

 Draw an important event from the story.

 Look at the pictures on page 4 and pages 13–17.

 Talk about things in the garden that are real and not real.

 Draw and **write** about something real or not real.

Listen to and **look** at pages 24-25.

 Talk about how the author helps you imagine flowers and strawberries at night.

 Draw and **write** your ideas.

The flowers and strawberries look like

_____

- -

_____

Find Text Evidence

 Read to find out what Hop can do.

 Underline uppercase letters in the title.

Hop Can Hop!

I am Dot.

I like Hop.

Shared Read

Find Text Evidence

Circle and read the word **my**.

Underline two words that rhyme on page 21.

I am hot.

See my hat on top!

Hop is hot.

Hop can hop on top.

Find Text Evidence

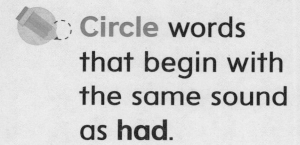

Read and point to each word on this page.

Circle words that begin with the same sound as **had**.

Hop can hop, hop, hop.

I can hop, hop, hop!

Shared Read

 Find Text Evidence

 Circle who can sip.

 Retell the story. Reread if you do not understand something. Use the pictures to help you.

I can sit.

Hop can sit.

Pop and I can sip.

Hop can sip.

Listen to the poem "The Seed." Look at the picture. What plant parts grow from a seed?

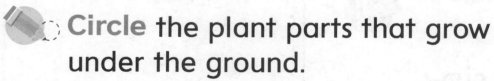 **Circle** the plant parts that grow under the ground.

 Draw boxes around the plant parts that grow above the ground.

Quick Tip

Talk about the plant parts using these sentence starters:

The plant parts that grow under the ground are _____.

The plant parts that grow above the ground are _____.

Listen to the poem again.

 Talk about the rhythm and words in the poem that rhyme.

 Draw a picture of the word that rhymes with *seed.*

Write About It

Think about the poems you read about seeds and plants. Write a poem about a plant or a garden.

Parts of a Plant

Step 1 **Talk** about different parts of a plant.
Choose two plant parts to learn about.

Step 2 **Write** a question about these
plant parts.

_____

- -

_____

_____

- -

_____

Step 3 **Look** at books or use the Internet.
You can use a picture dictionary
to look up words you do not know.

Step 4 Draw and **write** about what you learned.

Step 5 Choose a good way to present your work.

Mary, Mary, Quite Contrary

Mary, Mary, quite contrary,
How does your garden grow?
With silver bells and cockle-shells,
And pretty maids all in a row.

Hughes, Herbert, Mother Goose. "Mary, Mary, Quite Contrary." In *Rhymes Set to Music*, vi. London: Boosey and Company, 1913.

 Talk about the things that grow in this nursery rhyme.

 Think about the things that grow in *My Garden*.

 Compare the gardens.

Quick Tip

You can use these sentence starters:

The garden in the nursery rhyme _____.

The garden in the story _____.

Draw What a Plant Needs

1 **Think** about the texts you read. What did you learn about what living things need to grow?

2 **Draw** what a plant needs to grow.

3 **Label** your picture. Use words that you learned this week.

Think about what you learned this week. Turn to page 11.

Build Knowledge

? Essential Question **How do living things change as they grow?**

Build Vocabulary

 Talk about how living things change as they grow. What words tell about how living things change as they grow?

 Draw a picture of one of the words.

Write the word.

_____

- -

_____

My Goals

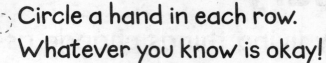
Circle a hand in each row.
Whatever you know is okay!

What I Know Now

I can read and understand texts.

I can write about the texts I read.

I know how living things change as they grow.

Key

 I understand.

 I need more practice.

 I do not understand.

 You will come back to the next page later.

Circle a hand in each row. It is okay if you need more practice.

What I Learned

I can read and understand texts.

I can write about the texts I read.

I know how living things change as they grow.

Retell the nonfiction text.

 Write about the text.

One important fact is

_____

- -

_____

 Text Evidence

Page

The most interesting part is

_____

- -

_____

 Text Evidence

Page

- -

_____

Talk about a tree you have seen.

 Draw and **write** about the tree.

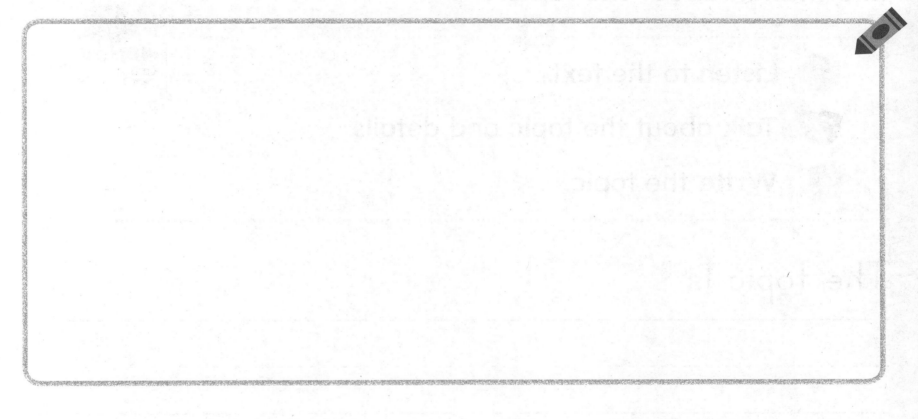

This tree

_____

- - - - - - - - - - - - - - - - - -

_____

The **topic** is what a nonfiction text is mostly about. **Details** in the words and pictures give information about the topic.

 Listen to the text.

 Talk about the topic and details.

 Write the topic.

The topic is

Draw two details that tell about the topic.

1.

2.

Check In

Listen to and **look** at pages 6-7.

 Talk about words the author uses. How does she make the tree seem like a person?

 Write your ideas.

The tree is like a person because

_____

- -

_____

_____

- -

_____

Look at the shape of the words on page 29. How does the shape help you picture the trees?

 Talk about why the author put the words on the page in this way.

 Draw one of the trees.

Find Text Evidence

 Read to find out about Ed and Ned.

Underline words that begin with the same sound as **end**.

Ed and Ned

Ed is not a pet.

Ned is not a pet.

Shared Read

 **Find Text Evidence**

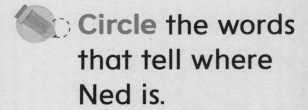 **Circle** the words that tell where Ned is.

Underline words that have the same middle sound as **hen**.

Ned is up, up, up.

See Ned! See Ned!

Janette Hill/Alamy

Ed met Ned.

Ned met Ed.

🔍 Find Text Evidence

✏️⋯ **Underline** words that begin with the same sound as **egg**.

✏️◌ **Circle** and read the word **Are**.

Ed can sip, sip, sip.

Ned can sip, sip, sip.

Are Ed and Ned hot?

Are Ed and Ned wet?

Shared Read

 **Find Text Evidence**

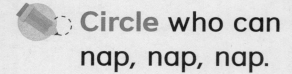 **Circle** who can nap, nap, nap.

Retell the text. Use the words and photos to help you.

Ed can hop, hop, hop.

Raimund Linke/Photodisc/Getty Images

Ned can nap, nap, nap.

a seed

The seed
sprouts.

a seedling

a sapling

 Talk about the diagram. What can we learn about how apples grow?

 Underline the label for the seed.

 Circle the plant parts that grow when the seed sprouts.

Quick Tip

You can use these sentence starters:

The seed will _____.

The seedling will _____.

Listen to page 34.

 Talk about the diagram. How does it show what a seed needs to sprout?

 Write about two things a seed needs to sprout.

A seed needs

_____

1. _____

_____

2. _____

Talk About It

How is a diagram helpful for learning about how an apple seed changes as it grows?

How Trees Grow

Step 1 Talk about different kinds of trees.
Choose two kinds to learn about.

Step 2 Write a question about these trees.

_____

- -

_____

_____

- -

_____

Step 3 Look at books or use the Internet.

Step 4 Draw what you learned. Add labels.

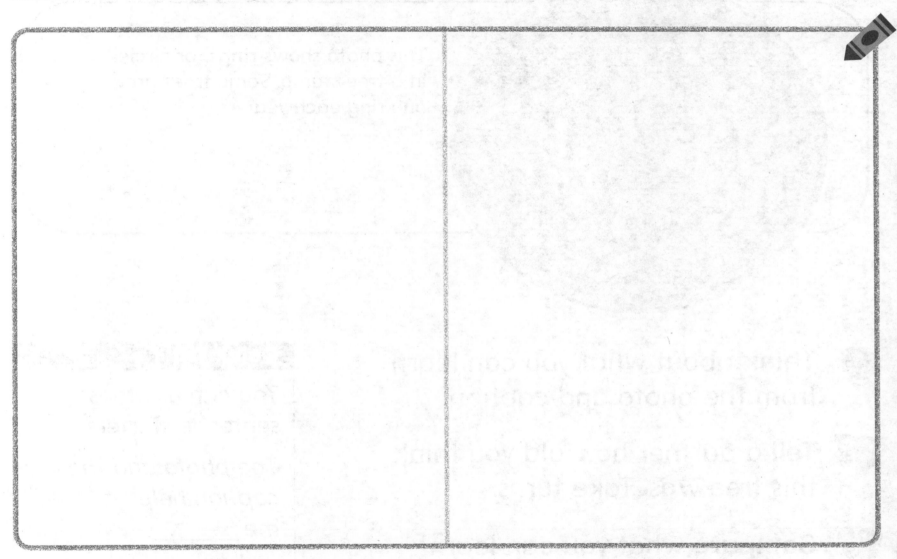

Step 5 Choose a good way to present your work.

Make Connections

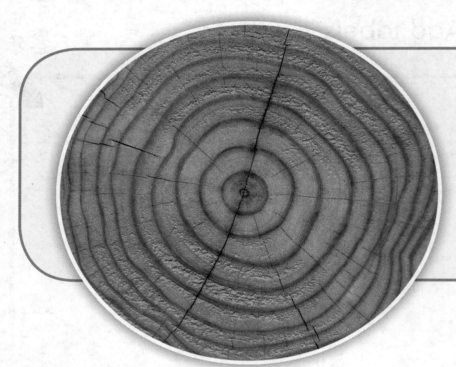

This photo shows **rings**, or circles, in a tree stump. Some trees grow one ring each year.

 Think about what you can learn from the photo and caption.

 Tell a partner how old you think this tree was. Take turns.

 Compare what you can learn from this photo to what you read about trees this week.

Quick Tip

You can use these sentence starters:

The photo and the caption help me _____.

I think the tree was _____.

Imagemore/Glow Images

Draw How a Plant Grows

① **Think** about the texts you read. What did you learn about how living things change as they grow?

② **Draw** how a plant changes as it grows. What part grows first? What part grows next? Draw the steps in order.

③ **Label** the steps. Use words that you learned this week.

Think about what you learned this week. Turn to page 35.

Build Knowledge

Essential Question What kinds of things grow on a farm?

Build Vocabulary

 Talk about foods that grow on a farm. What are some words that name these foods?

 Draw a picture of one of the foods.

 Write the word.

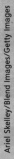

My Goals

Circle a hand in each row.
It is important to do your best.

What I Know Now

I can read and understand texts.

I can write about the texts I read.

I know the kinds of things that grow on a farm.

Key

 I understand.

 I need more practice.

 I do not understand.

 You will come back to the next page later.

Circle a hand in each row.
Keep up the good work!

What I Learned

I can read and understand texts.

I can write about the texts I read.

I know the kinds of things that grow on a farm.

Retell the nonfiction text.

Write about the text.

One important fact is

_____

- - - - - - - - - - - - - - - - - -

_____

Text Evidence

Page

The most interesting part is

_____

- - - - - - - - - - - - - - - - - -

_____

 Text Evidence

Page

- - - - - - - - - - - - - - - - - -

_____

Talk about foods in your store
that come from farms.

 Draw and **label** one of these foods.

This food is

_____

- -

_____

The **topic** is what a nonfiction text is mostly about. **Details** in the words and pictures give information about the topic.

 Listen to the text.

 Talk about the topic and details.

 Write the topic.

The topic is

_____

- -

_____

_____

- -

_____

Draw two details that tell about the topic.

1.

2.

Talk about how the pictures on pages 20–21 show what the trip was like.

 Draw one place from the trip.

The trip

_____

- -

_____

Look at the picture on pages 30–31.

 Talk about what other things are "bursting with the seasons inside" like the orange.

 Draw and **label** some of them.

Read to find out what Ron and Red do.

Circle and read the word **with**.

Ron With Red

Ron is with Red.

Red is a pet.

Shared Read

🔍 **Find Text Evidence**

✏️ **Underline** and read the word **He**.

✏️ **Circle** the word that begins with the same sound as **fed**.

Red can see a 🐦.

bird

Can Ron see it on top?

Dad can see ten .
oranges

He can fit ten in a .
basket

Shared Read

Find Text Evidence

Circle words that begin with the same sound as **rat**.

Underline words that tell where the bird is.

Red can see a 🐦.

bird

Can Ron see it on top?

Mom can see ten .
tomatoes

Mom can fit ten on top.

Find Text Evidence

 Read and point to each word in the sentences on page 73.

Retell the story. Look at the pictures if you do not understand something.

Ron can sit and sip.

Red can see a .

bird

Ron did not see a .
bird

Red can see it on top!

Look at the photos. What do they tell you about ways farmers sell their foods?

 Circle one way farmers sell foods nearby.

 Draw a box around one way foods travel to places far away.

Quick Tip

You can say:

One way farmers sell their foods is _____.

One way foods travel is _____.

Talk about ways farmers can sell their foods.

Write about two ways farmers can sell their foods.

Farmers sell foods

_____

- -

_____

Farmers sell foods

_____

- -

_____

_____

_____

Talk About It

Look at pages 36–37. How is the information shown on these pages different?

Plants on a Farm

Step 1 **Talk** about plants that grow on a farm. Choose one to learn about.

Step 2 **Write** a question about the plant.

_____

- -

_____

- -

_____

Step 3 **Look** at books or use the Internet. Look up words you do not know. You can use a picture dictionary.

Step 4 Draw and write about what you learned.

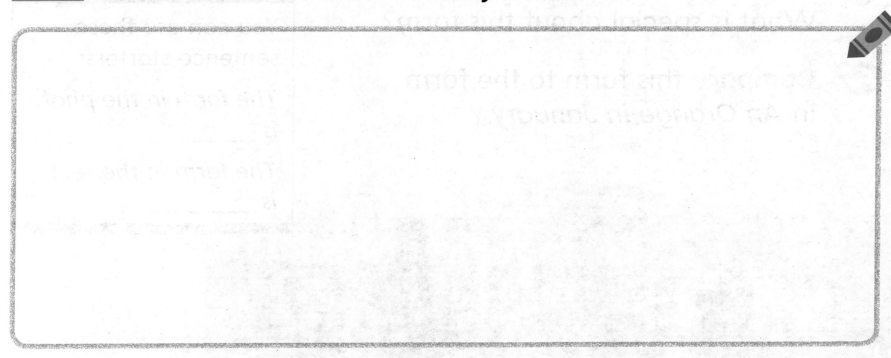

I learned

_____

_____

Step 5 Choose a good way to present your work.

Talk about the farm in the photo. What is special about this farm?

 Compare this farm to the farm in *An Orange in January*.

Quick Tip

You can use these sentence starters:

The farm in the photo is _____.

The farm in the text is _____.

This community farm grows on a rooftop in the city.

julief514/iStock/Getty Images

Make a Shopping List

1 Think about the texts you read. What did you learn about the kinds of things that grow on a farm?

2 Draw a list of foods that you can buy at a farmers' market.

3 Label the foods. Use words that you learned this week.

Think about what you learned this week. Turn to page 59.

Think About Your Learning

Think about what you learned in this unit.

 Share one thing you did well.

 Write one thing you want to get better at.

_____

- -

_____

- -

_____

Share a goal you have with your partner.

My Sound-Spellings

Aa apple — a	**Bb** bat — b
Cc camel — c ck k	**Dd** dolphin — d
Ee egg — e	**Ff** fire — f
Gg guitar — g	**Hh** hippo — h_
Ii insect — i	**Jj** jump — j
Kk koala — c k ck	**Ll** lemon — l
Mm map — m	**Nn** nest — n
Oo octopus — o	**Pp** piano — p
Qq queen — qu_	**Rr** rose — r
Ss sun — s	**Tt** turtle — t
Uu umbrella — u	**Vv** volcano — v
Ww window — w_	**Xx** box — x
Yy yo-yo — y_	**Zz** zipper — z _s

Aa Bb Cc Dd Ee

Ff Gg Hh Ii Jj

Kk Ll Mm Nn

Oo Pp Qq Rr

Ss Tt Uu Vv

Ww Xx Yy Zz